MW01659867

60

L. Michael Cheek

PublishAmerica
Baltimore

First printing

PublishAmerica has allowed this work to remain exactly as the author intended, verbatim, without editorial input.

ISBN: 1-60474-743-9
PUBLISHED BY PUBLISHAMERICA, LLLP
www.publishamerica.com
Baltimore

Printed in the United States of America

Dedication

To Ben, Lucas, Jaclyn, Rebecca and the ever patient Susan.

15 Minutes

She crochets in a corner chair
A fabric delicate and precious
as blue fingers on sleeping eyes

Beneath the ashes coals
barely breath
a snore or two
To disturb the coverlet of powder

Before time begins, the snooze button
bargains moments
stolen from calamity,

Sharks and barracudas can wait
My harpoon's edge is not yet sharpened
For 15 minutes of delayed
Ambition, an opera of growing grass

all the time I can't explain
these stolen minutes are mine.

A Letter from Dad

Each loop and slash familiar as a face,
addressed in the moment
of the pendulum's arrested sweep.
For a reluctant heartbeat
the mail slot yawns
bottomless, without end.
The metal slaps. Falling leaves echo.
The floor meets the ceiling.

What is writ would never be read
save for a stamp and a postmark.
This time, this date
inconvertible as a knife stroke,
final as final steps.

The page will not sleep.
A day, a week, however long it takes.
The words can wait.
It doesn't matter anymore.
The last letter from a dead man
Closes with a bitter good bye.

A Spring Warmed Rock

Table wine and cheese
Crush of needles
A fragrant lay.

The soil swarms millions
Ladybugs stupored by the unexpected sun.
There is but one path
From the caskets of winter
Through the shade of matted needles.
We gather by the armfuls, her naked grove of hair
Exploring legs, encased wings to virgin flight.

An Answer to Your Poem

You say you want the constellation, the sum of suns
fires to warm, fires to temper,
fires for the crucible between your legs.
Your pencil intones the page like a frost
clappered bell buoytelling the falling tide,
the hidden rock.
    Why fancy the stellar Bedouin?
    You are intertidal with liquid contours,
    salt leavened, lunar marled,
    uncertain.
Lay to rest this rough bubble,
this blistered romance and trembling.
Your poems are white horses
passing trackless through mist.

An Exchange of Cards

Strangers never seek eye contact.
But I look
For the frame hidden behind
The shell of years.
I see eyes that remind of morning fires
and the nourishment of honeyed hair.
Going down the up escalator.

Her face changes from traveler's anxiety
To the vague desperation of placing
The face all the while
Both hands in tow
To awfully familiar children.

What is it about that man's
bent smile that stops
Her tongue mid throat
and stammer

Yes No, Yes No
Confirmation of pillow dialogue
Years and marriages and children ago.
His hand spins a sign. She mouths
Words in the din of planes to catch.

The escalator never stops
A continuous conveyor of feet
Until a leaping and landing
And sprawling into space.

Space is what we wanted then
And grows more vast with each
Stranger crowding behind.
Is she waiting somewhere below?
Have I time? Damn.
This flight is important to me.

But is she waiting? Have we time,
Have we the space in this anxious
corridor to say hello and repeat
At one another the questions of life
these past 10 years?

Maybe an exchange of cards
She dropping for a moment the lively
pink fingers in her clutch
To grope in her handbag
For a sliver of card stock
Announcing her new name.

But is she there?

Would the card be enough reminder
To call sometime, either of us
Or detritus that stares
from the bottom corner of the drawer
while we try to remember how it got there.

Would we have time to talk
Share a cup, introduce her children
But no, I have to make this flight
and into space it is announced.

Anaesthesia

Sleep, my children, sleep and hope to wake
Share the dreams left to share
Share each shared pulse as one
Share no more tomorrow

Compromise makes weary
this crowded Universe.
Which of us, dear sister,
could live content with primacy,
which one subdue sorrow.
The scalpel cuts both ways with one stroke.

A penny in the well to walk upright,
nose through corridors of grass,
crawl in the dust, swim.
I want to swim.
I want to go left instead of right.
Choose instead of fingered by fate.

We know how lovers revolt
From tiresome intimacy
        And who could forget
Crippled smiles and legions
of stunned expressions.

Even spent leaking blood onto the pillow
The price is right for a day without bondage,

A Trunk of Archives

One clapboard shack at a time
sharecroppers with huge sore hands,
sons as weary and as hollow
stiffened for the wandering artisan
and bought immortality for a dime.

Archives curl around the penciled
names of starched old women holding babes,
brass visioned young men in stiff uniforms,
maids blurred by dust and reunions
of forgotten faces.

What lines can be read between
threads of ribbon around hair locks,
yellowed obituary of the purged branch
made tidy with tears.

    Eve's duty treasured names born and dead
    progeny spawned year after year
    her medley of labor and hard labor,
    her hands, her crochet, her womb,
    Her archives of all she wanted
    remembered, her chronicles without stain.

Oral histories censure storms of civic
    Spirit conspired in soil shed from thumbed Bibles.
Indictments infect the disquiet of Sunday dinners.
If no one speaks, societies of rope and midnight justice
can be carried safely to the grave.

Assisted Living Does Not Allow

Loud noises, food in the rooms
Lights on after lights out,
Cohabitation of life mates,
Objects more complex than blunt scissors,
More than three showers a week,
Children,
Singing.

The administration knows the limits of license
Needles to serve, services to call
If a resident refuses food and water
And wants no more assistance to live.

Shining

Comb over types believe the wind will behave
And spare cherished trivia,
The tattered trophy of an extinct crown.
Standing straight up or fopped over,
No amount of bravado is worth the crow.

Those of us skinned alive
Weather the lumps genetics dealt
with as much aplomb as frost allows and
suffer the wind until the discovery
The hat does indeed make the man.

Bering Sea

This sea is a stallion rarin' to buck
rarin' to kick butt to bulkhead, rarin'
to fling top heavy crabbers into troughs
of panic and submission. It charges
land like an broken fence and tears
at sand roaring foam, slinging
kelp and detritus, nets, abandoned
treasures and adipocere saints
searching the sky.

During spring bloom the sea bleeds green. Cumuli of pollock
spawn form thunderheads in the tide. Shearwaters feed
in frenzies of ten thousands. But the Bering Sea has no
manners, like a wealthy grand dame who greets
guests with oily grace then throws hot coffee
in their laps and cold water in their face.

Waking from under ice, the sea is restless,
Impatient to kick loose harness and riggin', eager
to breed storms and graze upon the foolish
who dare ride blinded by streaking mane
and none may rest
and none may sleep
except of nightmares and wild horses.

Beware, Traveler

Shismareff, 2003

The sand sprouts ancestries, unfashioned residues
Scoured wood, bones, many bones and newer metal
Seal, walrus and human pieced together behind one mask.

In spring evenings old women stalk the beach grass,
Gathering loaves and fishes
Where sea ice moans against the slit of land.

The sea spews sand. The sand drifts.
The heartbeat of elder time
Subtle as dancing drums.

The hunter marches into the sea sky,
Where the land sky and the ice breed mirages
And disappears in a squint of tears.

This one place they've clung to the equilibrium of sand
Between lagoon and crumbling sea,
Between providence and the famine of failure

Racks of flesh blacken in the wind
Open graves of rancid oils
Render an understood coinage.

Blood Rights

The scissortail snatches on the wing
nervous fluff boiled from the pasture
    beyond her martin house,
    empty now these five years
Since I buried her and the hole alongside
Waiting.

The dark fruit of living too long.
Just as well an awkward mass
should liberate my loneliness.
Let it flourish in this tired red soil like
the beans and okra in our garden
    Every stab of fire
    Brings comfort.

    The Stepchildren

They tramped the old house
seizing disporia: a child's gift,
installments of cookware,
the decomposing letters of a lost son,
a dying old man shuffled to a trailer.

Twas we whose mother wifed him 40 yrs
Whose one picture, the prating logic of blood
Allowed him, alongside children we'd never seen
Sure, death comes to us all.
He is country enough to bear the knowledge
Of his last baseball game and smile when asked
Even if it hurts.
Can we trust to compassion for a last drink of water?

The Nephew and his Wife

He ain't doin no good. Caint do
Nothin' for hisself, sitting in that musty old house.
So, Me an Robby barryed a pickup,
went down there and moved him.
Jes like that.
Hit was time. Cleaned the whole place out.
One of them daine girls called jes as we was leaving.
Boy, was she surprised.

He's pretty comfortable out back. Got his own privacy, that's
The way he is you know. Not wanting to be a burden to nobody.
We feed him. He's got his old cheer and TV and hit
Ain't so hot he needs air conditionin.
Phone calls from them others wanting to visit wid him
Even comin all the way from Texas like we was
Obliged to let 'em in.

Putting Down Brutus

This snow: frazzled remnant,
infinitely delicate.
This moon: a nameless monument,
implacable witness
gleaming through brambles of frost.
Listening to the last exploded thought.

An incense of burnt powder sulks
among beards of lichen.
Magpies tremble behind
the secrecy of wings
On this night: this fallen shroud,
such a shroud of stone that
tiny hard pebble: my heart.

This darkness has neither mercy nor patience
and betrayal is no time for joking, this thorny weight, these
crippling scars, swift dead wings: ultimate self torture.

But no,
nobody fouls my dirty work.
What a small sound
the left barrel made.

Consummate Flag

A winter willow brushed
the windshield in a lovers' view of the river.
Night without boundaries,
slow frolic of vapors,
moon's icy columns
greet a new woman.

The naked willow bends under
becoming laces, unlaced hooks
uplifted wires, handfuls of cups
A proud wound borne privately
save the boast of this flag.

The willow witnessed the impatient
trembling across thresholds, across
voids of doll's eyes, the eclipse
of a father pierced by precious needles.
Cries of hiemal jubilation, of triumph.

Notes to My Daughter

You cried when I woke you from your nap.
small in the fabric of my arms
squirming into that place
where curtains inhale dreams.
I can't hold you long enough. Forever
would never be enough.
Your breath is warm.

D'Boss

Up at four, buttdragging home around eight
dogdamned tired from growling all day,
pissing out territory, taking the gamble.
The big gamble because winning
is worth killing envy.

Losers are serfs, just average.
The average man ain't hungry enough to lay his money
Down to the expectations of brass balled bankers.
or compete with arsenals of deceit,
or pander to goddam bureaucrats
with little to do but strut in sinecure legions.

The employees. You can't get good help these days,
show up drunk, and salesmen believe hustle is a drag.
Customers think it's charity.
Winning is worth losing trinkets of tolerance
until nothing is left but the drive to win
and the torn tongue of the adding machine.

The salvation of quitting admits defeat.

You want success?
Thicken your skin, exorcise mercy to cold storage.
An average insult has not the boorish authority
to wilt a mother with shame.
The average disgrace does not redden employees to rage
juggling bills and gelded by fruitless sparrings
to heel and toe the unemployment line
and face the kids after school.

Remind them who's boss
and who's jack shit.

Kick some goddamned ass.
Be a leader of men. Embrace the addictive rush,
testosterone at its best. Hell,
just do it 'cause you can.
Then take it home and lash out at the children,
more powerless still-a certain justice to that-
until they grow a belly full and quit in frustration.

Berate the wife,
test her tolerance of command
then buy her a present-just enough
to show off the winnings but not enough
to forgive the imperfection of her years.
Only success has friends.
Failure is a sorry orphan.
Vision needs just one beholder
and by god no discussion of who's
in charge of this whole sonofabitch

Dear Skits

Remove the head remove
the arm
remove the wound between
her legs
The sanity of man is senseless.
They don't know what fun they're
missing.
I do not see you
no
I do not see you
at all.

The Dolphin's Daughter

She came on the crest of gale foam
gasping the breath of fishes
through the mouth of man.
Land's half and a half from the sea,
a freak in the Garden of Eden.

Ashimera ashimeri aglissle
Estrous body salt lustered
tempest pounded smooth and firm
swift from fatherhood's legacy, his reckless
intrusion into seductions from land,
her mother's lover of water
giving spawn to this allurement
in the trampled crush of genes

Arresting vision, the dolphin's daughter
reared in sun drumming sea shadows,
the wild and unforgiving sea.
She sings her siren's song.
        Lame on land, the sailor
Glides out to meet her.

Drinking

Drinking, what's my drinking?
there's nothing shrong with me
just 'cause i suck down a few beers
and brood out the window
full long past brimming.
Brown muses meander through cobwebbed galleries.
Day dreams pause for a dillettante's
examination of some quaint mental quirk.
Lookers and not buyers.   Pass to the next absurdity.
Refill the glass.

Behind a barred door
Authorized Personnel Only
A hallway of regrets
slithering over one another.
Dreaded memories from the cesspool
slinging buckets of shame and recrimination.
Ah shit   Take a sip.

Oh, look at all those petty
ambitions apuppering like mackerelies
about a bit a bacon.
Fantasies reel and unwound.
Berserk beasties breed another drama.
Day dreams in the gallery
Disparage abstruse abstractions
Have another.

The Easiest Woman in Texas

Simon sez, jump little Lisa.
Boy, could little Lisa jump.

The night bristled eyes for only Lisa
as did day, especially morning when
her skin delighted the sun on the pillow
and flowers beseeched rain on Spanish mesa.

Llano estacado winds would lift her skirt
and sweep men to fits of fainting,
arouse in shy souls stallion dreams
and excite the proud to acts of shame.

To say that Lisa was beautiful
would reduce Venus to mere hagdom
and that little Lisa could connive
distill the ocean's volume to a hatful.

A man might argue that he could
resist the swell of her breasts,
the urgent ache of loin
But never in her prairie moon, never her lips.

The dry moors of mesquite thorns
green spines of yucca, lean and always
hungry, a challenge to water
a calling of dust in the wind.
Her voice made rages of clouds.

How many tried to confine
the storms she brewed.
The souls sold for another taste.
The bones broken in the trample.

Barium Enema

Eah. Again.
The fifth seat from breakfast,
round imprint of mulled disquiet
that all ain't right along the gurry pipe.
Magnesium citrate endowed my bowel
with a mind of its own
and once freed of the daily schedule
lapsed lazy, lawless, shameless,
as flaccid and tedious as sausage skin.

It is wise to be chary of the technician's dull wit
whose determined insertions require
unflinching curiosity and distracting chitchat.
Since when is a wee gut ache prophecy?
Will I die stoppered up
without the rank pleasures of morning privy
to muster thoughts strayed in the night?
Should I submit, removing all doubt
Confirm the need for denial?

Statesmen, poets, idolized divas
whether hairy, shriveled, dainty or smooth
all look alike in the narrow elements.
All engage the bung balloon tight lipped,
Condemned by barium's shadow
to the validations of television
without benefit of color commentary
or the comic appeal of flatulence.

Gurgling tide pools blink into the gamma sun
But where are the polyp's coral engravings?
There is nothing here.
There is nothing beyond the diagnosis
of each morning's bouquet and the contented
narcissism of fine workmanship.
There is nothing but the glad-eyed stumble
across the gulf between diaper and grave.

Fishing Naknek

The fisherman can only hope
his special rites win favor
        among windrows of creeping salt.
Here, eternal faith is ordinary vision
because science eludes places where rocks have names.

The exalted lay before the altar
colorful sacrifices, enticing superstition,
feathers to embellish steadfast belief.
The next offering will appease those feverish goddesses
enthroned in showers of light and scales
deep in the current of grasses
and if not,
then the next, or next after,
maybe.

In soft or strumming rain, Eyes glazed
By gluttony of perfect water,
Dreamers cast upon the dream
and lay small bets on the outcome.

Haying Time in Little Horn Country

My green seas swell
beneath the darting blackbird.

I'm going farmin', jacket in hand
worn and ragged from days of sunshine
leaving you to wash brown rivulets
from the brink of my cup.
Patience girds my labors.
Endowments of dust sustain me.
I drive to move the mountain's water
and soak my fields with light.

I love you.

I chase the Indian's horses from the south meadows
and fix that damned fence, wave bent old George
working the swather and watch
a weasel slither through cut alfalfa
to the hot blood of young pheasants.

My shirt sticks. I leave my jacket in the truck.
A hawk attempts the sky.
Blackbirds drive off the intruder.

Home

I'm going to fix it up
Someday I'll make it shine
Haul the crap off
Fix the cracked retaining wall and repaint
Finish the trim, plumbers and the like
Someday.
For now I'll leave the peas cascading the wall
The snapdragons smothered in wildflowers
Some folks call weeds
And the rhubarb thick and red,
The cat flattened on her belly
Her tail hot.
This creation has some awfully funky parts:
The porch that sticks out like a broken leg
The hiddy hole of walls inside, the shop that isn't
Used enough
But my toe of land dips into the Tanana River.
Sandpipers leave not a ripple you can see.

Canto

Where grows the tree that shed
leaves on mirrors of oiled water?
Who wove this carpet of glass?
Whose signature this repose of cardboard?
How long endured the fists of wind
in narrow dead ends smudged with smoke.

Could this memory be
a face of stone, rimed with lime of doves
Surely
something lingers beyond the thread of days
some stray aroma of hair seducing the past,
Some encysted remnant of ring or metal.
Surely more than pariah's breath
kissed with decay?

The rectangles of sky come hissing down
on the corners of commerce
where the perfumed ranks wait,
Parched commas in every eye stare
everywhere but here.
Take a chance on a look,
look
within the span of a heart, a single breath
look
where you could be
not me.

I Never Expected This

My boys bend over ants,
sprouting seeds, furtive tadpoles
hair never combed, a mess
to their own balding age.
Never mind me
holding down
this hot bubble to realize
that love could be such suffering.

Seeking the Light in November

Eighty trains a day and night blaze through Woodward,
Oklahoma, the urgent pulse of industry, grain
and containers, and trailers and treasures
from terminal to coast terminal, a frenetic
thunder, an assurance that the here and now is
as important as what was.

The hospital window looks on the tracks
on the oak trees and the ash trees, on the brown lawns,
into the sun reflected from other windows.
The town wakes, surprised it seems
that dawn could fill our time
That dawn could catch resigned voices
in the hallways between dreams and delirium.
That dawn could find the pump still wheezing like a reluctant heart.
Another drop of food, another day.

He started at 15 he said, when we could speak
of the unbroken caravan of camels
into 60 years of smoke,
of the blinding country that was youth, how the spirit of our hands
is the remembrance of our labor,
and burning matters said out of the hearing of women.

    I attended the night, with the night shift, with Nancy,
Claudine, and the others who have watched
and tended this way before.
Little could be done and little
could be said, and little could be said
without choking on salt and ashes.

At times he was a father, infallible, a superman who repaired
what was broken, who left unsaid what need not be spoken.
Now, in the ponderous silences he remembers
the sprinkler needs fixing and seed for the birds
while the mirrors of the soul reflect
A holocaust of bone and melted flesh
and the traceries of nerves become highways of flame

The final fever cools. The final goodbyes reach into
the measureless oceans of morphine
retreat like waves, tremulous
in the advancing light.

Leonard's Story

Old timers tell their stories hunkered
Over coffee and spitting brown into a can.
Deer hunting and fishing too good to be true.
Dragging a crawfish net and coming up leaves
And the blue bottle there on the shelf.

Old timers had it easy, so they say.
Blunt force of chores to keep
A father's belt where it belonged
And Germany and Japan and young
Men gone defined the day.

Old timers tell their histories
without subtleties of hidden meaning.
Unwritten stories taken at face
Without the dissections of desperate academics
Who must write something if nothing at all.

Leonard's father kept turkeys,
A bird known for craft in the cottonwood bottom,
Wild grain rippled with lordly old gobblers,
Serene harems, strings of obedient chicks,
Boys with 22's duped and beguiled.

Leonard can see the hawk screen,
how the gnats boiled torpid smoke
through webs of wire, feed sacks wringing dust,
how the white mist of homebred turkeys tarred the air,
Leonard can hear still the eager cluck of a thousand voices.

By his father's will, Leonard
fed them and shoveled the pen.
Water from the trays uplifted in their throats.
The first keen pink ear proclaimed the thunder,
a sky of miraculous gods.

Exalted the flocks of B-17s
Training the take-offs of war.
The squabble of pecking politic paled in comparison.
The first word of adoration, any explanation
For the wrath from heaven. Eyes skyward, voices awed.

Certainties they knew together surpassed
The doubt each knew alone.
Did not the gods roar and thunder,
gear down, catechisms of rotary engines?
So commanded, they followed.

Smothered in righteousness, piled against the fence
Leonard loaded the wheel barrow, 50 one day,
40 the next. Thinning rows of acolytes calling
for the gods to return and the everlasting moment
of grace made both whole and worthless.

Just Let Go

Let it be the volcano's cindered slope
Or an outward bend of the river
A private place with a view.
        Pray not
a bed wired to the stutter of my heart,
crowds of witnesses, the infinite sky of ceiling.
Pray not for those who use my dime
To test the limits of endurance.
        Let go.
I will not pray for immortality,
narcissistic ever after.
Living once is glory enough.
Let my dust vanish into swarms of fishes
Leave me be. Let me go.
Don't hold me back. Don't interfere.
Forget heroic palliatives. Forget the tears.
No time remains for vanity.
Just let go.

Manhunt

I
The Hunter

Tended only by God,
the sacraments of wild harvest,
exalting on sun bleached bluffs,
dark bottoms in riot, old orchards brooding fruit.
　　In the name of pheasants and quail,
　　in the cock's bold canticle of bright plumage,
　　I am blessed.
No song simpler than these twin throats
trembling aloft showers of hackle down.
No dance more joyful than the left foot leading
into weedrows, across quilts of broken corn,
through convolutions of steep
seed meadows the canyon shoulders inch by eon
above the river's muscular turquoise gems.

II
The Hunted

No one comes to the farther asylum
No one but a single hunter willing to balance
his secret down the mile or so of railroad rail.
A lathered man falling up the slope
pursued by a yoke of numbers
stands out like a bride's belly
in albedos of sweat and gasps
discordant with the hiss of seeds.

The paper said he escaped friday.
Two day's run from cages
saturated with distillations of body oils,
all eat, all stand, all sit
all voices clanging at all hours
all the interstices of space filled with faces, hands
all the blank indifference from all those walls.
Brought you to my sanctuary.

III
The Deputies

The truck followed a cow track to the water tank.
Horses stamped in the trailer.
The county's officers joked through gunsights and binoculars.
The radio squalled. They braced bootheels in the dust
and smoked against the hood. "Let him run," they said.
And he did until he ran out of cigarettes.

Middle Ages

It was only yesterday young women
bloomed rapt bouquets, musky tendrils
of swollen pudenda and fell mewling in their throats
for any old line, their melon bosoms and offerings of thighs.
Was it only yesterday?
The world's vast inventions sifting
like wheat grains through fingers,
a steadfast course on a destiny of great things,
tastes of emancipations melting on the tongue,
and the whole of the earth flowered into miracles
of imagination and fragrances.

Beyond hazy horizons
boundaries to the dreams:
the drain clogged with hair,
dry creak of oilless joints,
Old wounds reborn in burning glory.
The aspirations wrought from intricate vision:
wastelands of time's exacting conspiracy.
The arts of creation mildewed in dusty files.
Labor reduced to crepuscular waking and rising
into each morrow drained of bold vision
by a vampire's work of daily bloodletting.

At the edge of the eye, behind the left shoulder,
a shrew grins black triangular teeth
glossed with toxic saliva
always hungry, always compounding
interest in skinbound books accounting
images of ragged failures

unkept in dark corners,
sick moaning on wet couches,
gilt edged documents brown stained and curling,
bright endowments flaking rust and
passions splurged on fool's errands.

The bullet in the chest has a comfortable mass
or a knife sharp honed to a perfect point
of Japanese honor, a flat rock with a view
would be the ideal that has always escaped.
Only there's still the nest and this mess needs
picked up, maybe settle for less of the undone work.
Is the insurance paid?
Can the innocent be spared the residue?

Migraine

Lightning bulges the sky.
Archways and doorways dervish with leaves
Cobblestones crack under the weight of chariots
and chariot wheels clatter and spark.
Drums tremble the altars of goddesses
and lambs burn in the temples.

A cockroach of a man in a bird feather suit
spins a flint drill amid a jury of ravens.
Leagues of worms teem from his fingers
mouths itch for nervous delicacies.
He sutures with thorns of butterflies,
waits in corners for appointments with dust motes,
attends somber meetings called by ticks and mushrooms,
and studies into the night the arts of asymmetry.
He reads through wire nets with swollen eyes
and splits burls of bone in the altar's light.
The little cockroach commands magics of probe and vise,
compost and yarrow, hog's tusks and the stingers of hornets.
Skin drums bombard the temple chambers
beseeching the spirit released.

Moose Hunting

The contented mediate into flames.
The meat pole strains under shrouds
Partitioned flesh, seasoned with blood.

Time to indulge
In vices outside the critique
Of wife and children.
Quiet for one thing, listening and quiet,
Losing count of the days,
Rejoicing wild complines of cranes and geese
In their pilgrim's rollick. Birches
anointed by fog dripping one by one
showers of susurrus gold.

Spotting trees peer
over the backs of thickets
Branches scarred and oozing sap
onto the handsteps of years
Of watching the meadow grow.

Come nightfall
Crys in the darkness dent
the refuge of silence
Moans and grunts
Heard over the hiss and pop of fire.

I mend on a morning sit
Sounding bull calls and waiting
For the clap of plywood on the alders,
willow tops ransacked in tempests of lust,
Diadem spoiling from the brush.
Muzzle foaming, shoulders massive
And presenting that great neck
To my bullet.

My Hearing Is Not the Problem

I can hear rust flake from iron.
The chime of cilia eclipses meditations
and mannequins twitter behind glass.
The planet's spin comes through just fine,
Like a friction bearing searing its grease.

Clerks, cops, judges need reminding
What is obvious to them is the squabble of chickens.
In crowds and machinery, mouths muddle
Cobwebs fraught with nonsense.
The audiologist says deficits can be helped
But for five thousand bucks keys clang and
Cellophane wrappers crackle like thunder.

If the brain spills its harvest of kernels,
Essentials might bear repeating.
Speak clearly to the right ear.
It's somewhat better.
Telephones are a problem. Intrusive strangers,
Chances, polls and bagetelles
Invade my insular preferences.

.

Needle

l
o
ve
ly
pure
pier
cing
bliss
every
thing
else
means
nothing

Night Driving from Tok

Owl's light crawls up the stone washes
Licks, devours bare black roots.
Frost glint flirts branch to branch.
The sky's torn lip exhales rime.

Tracers gash delirium into the road.
White line fever, a fever for transport.

Lights race ahead,
climb the darkness, vanish
into the mountain's belly,
ghosts pursued by guitar and drum.

Rewind button found by touch
Favored storm of violin.
The melange of tapes,
Themes for wakefulness,
Reverie, remembrances.

Holly and Holiday
Short leashed, eager to fly,
The teens would never end.
But the *20s* were all as promised, without borders.
Should it be "Pretty Woman" for the 30s or "Only the Lonely"?
Should music be chronological or in order?
Don't forget thrice 4 times shy, burnt crispy on the outside,
still undone in the middle.

The trees harbor retinas. Phantoms of memories
Trotting into the cone of light.

The Onion Sackers

Will we always face another road,
another camp along an irrigation ditch
where the law can't find us or don't care.
Sleep comes sweet in the brown
cottonwood rain.

Will we always
know the certifications of our labors
sacks stapled and heaped and hauled away
in the truck track pressed into the dust.
Will our wages always tally on burlap.
Will our backs always
Bend into the harrowed earth, in sunburnt
haze of ashes, across infinitudes
one row at a time.

Will we always pack history beneath
our fingernails, our love making
Quick and weary,
our children into whatever schools
wherever the tilting world may find us.

Shall we always follow the fertile
crescents, the green bottoms of valleys,
to the head gates of all water
marking migration with cairns of the gleaning,
recording our miracles on a parchment skin.

Plenty of Time

I'll write that poem tomorrow.
There is plenty of time
To explore the sound of thought
And tomorrow or the day after
I'll get around to the unifying theory,
The essential fundamental hiding in daydreams
And meditations while driving.

There is plenty of time after all
To climb the list of mountains
hike the valleys and edges of water
Where tides of fragrances
Overwhelm and imprint
signatures of a lifetime.

Wake to verse, steamy ruminations o'r coffee
Window open to the measure of morning,
Crabapple straining against the bud.
There be plenty of time to herd cats,
organize worms, sort socks, make the bed
Be a hero, serve the master who enslaves.

One day I'll lose the paunch,
Resculpt the warrior, defuse frozen joints
Throw off the glasses and see the edges
Of the world clearly defined
Unencumbered by retrospection

Plenty of Saturdays ruined by Friday nights
Plenty of time to cradle an old head,
Gestures meant to last for the plenty of time
Between I love you and the vast silence
Trailing behind all that time.

Quittin' Time

We would never know the secrets
Appearances keep rigidly at bay.
Verity wraps itself in bubbles,
never a word betray.

The unmalleable actress
yields nary a sign
days on end, weeks on end,
forever.
Maybe during private times,
unguarded moments
the painfully gestated demeanor
May relax, may crack, may exhale
A hopeful whimsy unlike all others.

Search for sins forgiven or forgotten
The mold is shaped by
Bones of fate, burdens
built to last a lifetime

Reason cannot penetrate the etches of glaze
or the handiwork that shaped the bowl.
Reason cannot taste the multiplicity of flavors
that swirl like redemption in the hollows of soul.

Excuses pile upon excuses,
someone gets the blame.
Our rational self questions
who should pay and how much and
how long will be time enough
to pay for the eternity of this lifetime.

The clay is innocent.
You were eleven.

Sleeping to Rain

If ever there is rest
let it rain in dreams
Let the sky come loose
in tin drums
cadences of heart beats.
Let the air rise from its bath
earth scented
through open windows
Let cool
    inamorata
        lips
            kiss

Saturday Afternoon Nap

I push the truck seat back
The dome of my hat orbits constellations
Waves of breath scrape sand.
The breeze through the window is cool.

Seduction Gone Astray

Don't mess my hair she ordered
As if I could care less about the part
Of any hair except the part parted by
By exuberant labor

Do you think sex is talking about sex
I asked as plainly as a hot plate of hormones can ask
(this close to home is not a time for ambivalence)

Oh, I would tell any lie, whatever lie it took
Betray any custom, whatever custom needed betrayal
Profess homage and sincerity, write poems to weaken
The resolve of those clothed white thighs.

> Did she really believe coupling would be
> a gentlemanly trot through perfumed parks,
> diaphanous wings and birds singing
> As effortless as scratching any old itch?

Without joyous sweat and gurgling
Without earthquakes, incisions of crust
Without wounds to mark
My everlasting days.

Seeking Converts

The cabin still stands
though a craftsman never touched it.
Frost molded corners.
The floor whistled snow.
In brambles of rusted wire,
Ice screamed in the owl's night grip.
The window's hardened laces viewed
a narrow niche of the world.
Visitors weren't welcome in the deluge
of poetry spilled onto dried skins.
The door closed with bone and horn.

Come spring when grass buds
Saw through winter slag,
A hen covey of evangelics dared
Redeem the hearsay of dark gossip.
    Lord, be with us. Grace our venture.
    Guide our hand to rattle bones
    And summon from the lair's mouth
    The unrepentant challenge
    Clothed in hair and pheromone.

Pink to their white breasts, sweltering
marriages, inflamed in the unwashed
steam, undressed in a carnal gleam.
Tract and prophecy clutched like shields.
Their message cramped by animal
elements God created them to penetrate.
    A church-going woman knows trespass
    And the wreckage of earthy seductions.

But Lord, explain this ovarian ache low in the belly,
Rout of Sunday school virtues, the goading heat
The brooding soil, the grass buds noisy sawing:
Elements God created to penetrate.

Sharecroppers' Daughter

I was young, strong, happy.
I didn't know any better
than pinto beans, cornbread and poke salet.
Oh, we worked hard my sister and brother,
Mama rushing from the cotton rows to the stove,
Daddy brooding behind the team, lazy red tornadoes
splurting from the slow serenade of black hooves,
us kids, high on the wagon, laughing on the landlord's share.
He was a giant, my Daddy, but shrunken and scared
amidst the crop of invading tubes until,
at last,
the cancer choked him dead.
      Many things had changed by then
My own crop grown and headed with seed
But who had sown these disappointments?

Can you find me in front of Old Butler School?
We didn't know any better
than patched over coveralls and dresses white as flour sacks.
Those days teachers taught and by God we learned.
War came. The boys all left
their Mamas weeping in the dust and bus exhaust.
Some no account down the road claimed he was farming.
I knew better and turned the s.o.b. in. They drafted his sorry ass.
Got into a fist fight with him right
out on the front porch.
Daddy kept a gun by the door afterwards.
Mama always said I was the meanest of the lot
We didn't take crap from anybody.

Who was that man I married for 35 years? Whose crop have I
harvested? What landlord got the good share?
My own daughter gone crazy, my son over the horizon.

After I'd grown and left the halo
of Mama's oversight but not
the overflowing silo of her love
and met some veteran just back from Italy and Africa
who swept me away from my youth
and into (he thought) domestic servitude
did I come
to know any better.

Babies stop being babies eventually, so I went to work.
He swore and raged, but I wasn't raised
to depend on anybody. He gave me a crop
of shame from the gutter. I gave him a scorching from hell
but knowing any better still hurt.

Hurt and dragged down by obligations
of children and a vow like a green and tasseled crop
smothered in vines and suckers. That's the way it was
back then; a woman had no choice and I didn't
know any better. But I was learning.

He forged a business out of sheer will. I never a saw any man
work so hard. So I got in harness with him.
We made payroll, paid the bills, built something where
once there was nothing but
it didn't get any better.
When it was over, it was like I never knew him
but by then the best of the crop was gone.

Sunfishing

The snapping turtle hunkered in his pool
beneath the vault of oak and sycamore.
He ruled fishes and snakes, the errant muskrat.
A muddy shadow in the glimmer of water,
seated in his dominion of drifting leaves.

We bent under the rotting bridge
a twilight of cool echoes,
grasshoppers spitting in our fists:
sacrifices ghilliegouged for sunfish.

We fished our private cathedral from polished stones,
took blackberries from the thicket, respite from the heat.
Our floats plunged in a scurry of scales. Our lines
cut water. Our voices rang in the choir of trees.

He meditated through the intrusions,
aloof, dangerous, waiting in the solace of shell,
ancient jaws honed and hardened, sharp enough to sever bone,
dark in the heart of children who delighted in fingers
and dared wiggle toes in the July altar of water.

One day my bobber dove deep and hard,
weight slung heavy on the pole and the monster
seethed into the sanctum of air.
I dragged him to the gravel bar,
our din of triumph shattering the leaves.
Keith smacked his head with a piece of old board
'til that terrible white mouth smoked.
We left him baking in the sun, crows crying in the sycamores,

and walked home through a blaze of grasshoppers,
sunfish slapping at our legs,
struck dumb by ruin.

Surgery and Beyond

Follow the parade of pointed fingers
Along paths to private rooms.
No fever, no food, no water this past half day.
Chilled in the gown of moons.
Faces pop in, pop out. Are you ready?

The nurses have grown weary of gallows humor,
The wan composure of insects pinned to the board.
While cold infusions gallop
Whipped by the exacting heat of ivs.
    Whoa, that stuff comes on fast.

Nurses inventory pads and packaged medicals.
Nobody hesitates, nobody seems particularly busy.
Eyes peer down, crowd in.
Wait—perhaps put this off a while
The edges fold.
The ship pulls swiftly away.

Reincarnates waken to confusion and torment
with each soul possession of a different body.
The window's gray light pools on sweating tubes.
Truncheons of bandages hide the hours
Lost in artificial sleep.
What have I done? What have I done?

The Door Is Hollow

Swollen in the jambs,
Face whiskered by clawed splinters.
The knob is sticky as if some kid
With honeyed hands explored
closets he ought'n.

Once opened,
Damnations yawn a black
Magnetic mass. Once closed,
no light can penetrate
the cosmic dust.

The Singing Stone

Once, way off in the boonies
I found a boulder stone ringing
half buried, ringing such a fever
the ground hummed and tickled
my boot soles.
Where the hell am I, Black Curiosity?
Half rounded by some wandering river
gone rollicking in another bed,
half an encrustation of sharp edges
that cling to the skin like razors.
I talk. It answers,
sometimes so low I strain to hear
sometimes so high it whistles.
  The boulder stone has a message
but I only understand English and then rarely.
It's magic, I know that now,
sharing its squat view of the volcano
that flung it like fevered phlegm,
dazzling and frisky from torched crenellations.
I touch the razors and it bites.
I pat it's rounded buttocks and it whimpers,
licks my hand, all but rolls over for a brisk
rub on the belly.
I camp. I'm lost, more or less, anyway.
It's nice to have a companion.

The Miser's Funeral

The final sum of 30 thousand days
Renders a cold double line
spoken into a sleeve in the company
of strangers grateful for ceremony
and white wash.

Distillations of roses smother the unsaid.
Those who look below the sweetness
are seized by the nostrils
and shaken to horrid fascination
By the state of flesh.

To be the fly on the wall
Coolly stropping eye whiskers,
tonguing the air,
Maybe lay a thousand eggs or so
when no one is looking.

Nevermind the garlands of sums
Or the Mark in the garage
Or the ascendant swagger
Drifting like spider's web
On the shape of the wind.

The clock is a vulture
Breaking bones for the marrow
Stealing dentures and wallets
And schedules of pills.

Footsteps drown in gray carpet,
rooms a mute pastel.
The clink of coins cannot be heard.
Save for the tiny tinkling of a bell
One could forget it is a place of business.

There Was a Little Man

The little man slept in his little room,
Lived his little day under an open sky.
He had a sweat rimmed hat. Pants fluffed
Like sails of cloud around his little legs.
Such a little appetite:
A bite of biscuit, a bit of bacon.
It all tasted gray.

He hunched over his shovel, wheezed the earth
and water together. Thirsty roots drank, satisfied.

At night he coughed. Phlegm
Tangled in his throat. His skin waxed and waned
With the moon on the marred little mattress
For the first time he admitted,
a doctor might be worth the fee.

His nieces and nephews heard he'd never
Spent a dime, figured the frugal farm labor
maybe 10,000 in the bank.
They flocked to his side, perched on the chairs,
Cooed profitable words into his ear
And watched him die on the huge, white bed.

The Future of Time Travel

The new age thinks it's hot stuff
But time travel is not what it's touted to be.
It is enough to pass once without
the burden of confronting a younger oneself,
mere lamb obsessed with liberties,
heedless of all seasons save spring.
The adventurer is to the elder bag of aching joints
a shallow boor worthy of increased
disinterest after a moment's familiarity.

The Adonic proportions greeting each morning mirror
ill fit the glass nature has warped
and the view from either side is to view a stranger.
Would I nod to him at the post office?
Conversation beyond cursory is all but impossible.
There is little to say, even less understood
between claimants of a single soul.
What on one side is consequence, on the other flirtation;
one coltish, one reconciled; one mortgaged,

The other merely broke. One writes daring,
Experimental Poetry, the other pedantic, predictable, boring.
They have no friends in common, so aren't likely
to meet, but if perchance to face to face
each won't recognize the other
and may even come to blows.
Altogether, I think I'll stay.
He was a rude punk anyway.

To R

The roof mutes rain to hiss and
whisper, windows dripping, glinting gray
You lie bread quiet, slowly rising,
eyes closed pretending sleep. You have
a beautiful body.
　　On my elbow I watch you breathing, pulse
　　whetted on the dimpled plain of your belly,
　　the fine haired breasts that bewilder equilibrium,
　　smoldering heat from the cauldron of loin.
They open. I knew they would.
Your eyes are mischievous streams
where currents frolic amid cress and swimmer
and drag the drowning to rejoice.
　　Eager sharp teeth, tongue hungry
　　At your command, my brain nestles in warm tissues
　　Canyons and wrinkles whine with joy,
　　glands, secretions boiling, sparks fly
　　everywhere
Bidden to a garden of hidden paths, shy flowers,
a place to lie down on pillows of lichen
and clouds scented with sagebrush and heather
　　Your kisses slip to sweeten my ear, giddy
　　passion, an imperfect policy, deafens all else.
　　We fit perfectly.
　　lathered with sweat, pelvis frantic, demanding
　　my body, my sacrifice, my carefully saved semen.
The earth shudders. The world stops.
Gravity is sent reeling. Laws of physics are
prostrate in abeyance.
　　Your body smells healthy lying moist,
　　close, dew gathering in your eyes
　　while rain whispers on the roof.

R, Fini

Has you hair grown longer since I watched
your back turn Augusts ago
when love peered like a rooster in weeds
frozen by some brazen grasshopper in the dust?

In spite of your eyes, wind teasing the hay,
your reticent reluctance, my confounded confusion
won out in the end. So it finished,
a mule's kick in the heart.

Even after you had seeded
an enduring house,
I fancied your face etched in fog
and flying with fulmars over melancholy seas.

Even after all these Augusts, our separate tracks
split, decisive footprints on volcanic scoria
wander back in reckless memories
and mirages of silver splendor.

Even tarnished the silver is grand,
and the passion grown etiolated and unnourished
is exuberant memory of August meteors
and the spear you held to gut me.

Even October after cranes have lifted
proud dancer legs from lathered springs
I see your face, I smell your heat,
and wonder how you are.

But now, the birches bare, waiting snow
my lineage nested in sweat labor
The heart reconciles the memory.
The portrait freed of forty winters is put away.

A Walk in the Storm

No light no beacon no buoy belling,
no path no goal, only the millstone carried everywhere.
The sea does not whisper wind flogged invitations.
The sea has no equal for roaring and thunder,
for wrack and waste and indifferent carnage.
Carry the millstone to the bed of broken treasures.
You are too grave to be weightless.
This has its attractions
when letters are inadequate for the words beneath the words.

I hunker in a lee of sand and pull the thermos from my pack,
hold the steam beneath my breath,
and drink from the cup of dark reflections.
Escalades of sand swallow my tracks.
I am Nameless
among dunes anchored in the wind's limits,
in the swept arc of tattered rye:
torn banners in the vanguards of lemmings.

I tack from sand to sea,
Shout names into manes of foam.
Collisions of sea and sky
blur without boundaries.
A face makes itself in the squall
melts and reforms in the eyes of driven gulls.

Air of latent musk, poisoned salt
Of quick white serpents,
bones drained of marrow,
I walk the sand.

Walking on a Frozen River

The river closed three weeks ago.
slush scintered against rime in slow
exhalation of bitter smoke, the river seeking
final clarity amid crush and rumble.

It's firm enough now to cross
on a lawn of night growing frost.
Grazed by biting air, the ice squeals.

My boots sound like drums
in caverns written in roan oxen
and hunters with bows. I listen for
the river's deep green groan.

The Tanana shudders its back and spits
overflows of freezing fog, heaves hillocks
of exfoliating leaves and whispers cackling
jokes down bends of wandering.

All my surfaces are solid
They adhere each to another in one
cold armor. Beneath, in silent rushing,
I flow.

Watching the Storm

Cumulus nimbus,
Stratus mammiformus
Ferment and brooding eclipse the evening.

The imagination inhales deranged light
vast black herds of bison stampeding?
forges unseen, anvil and hammer,
scarcely a flick of an omnipotent finger.

Mother's milk untangles the trembling,
Invites the image carved in prancing shadows.
But demand exhausts the seer's science
though pages of equations
scatter in the trees' annoyance.

The mosquitoes' gallery
cannot waste the time
to contemplate the falling glass
but pester and frenzy the other world
for absolutions that never come.
The river flows. The rain stings.
Everything drips away.

Watering Twins

Mother planted petunias
blushed and pale blue to hug the porch
of the wee cabin where our conspiracy of love
blossomed into twins.
We both worked. I hammered together
another nest when I could.
There was much too much to do,
so the plants limped and perfume
shriveled to dusty vapor.

Saturday meant a full day on the new place
        but no
she needed to shop. "Water the flowers," she said and left.
My time, daylight burning, was too important
to watch kids and water friggin flowers.
I jerked the hose from the reel
cranked miffed muttering
Dust swallowed the shower.

My boys, twin heads fine as corn silk
leaned through my legs to clutch the marvel.
"Stand clear or you'll get wet" an invitation to creep closer
I slapped the spray and shocked their arms.
They shrieked to the honeysuckle
hands raised to praise the splendid sparticles.
giggled probes of Daddy's attention
dash under the arched spout
baby blond hair of water runnels,

diapers sagging, britches dragging
toddler feet slicking grass
a cloudburst as they hid behind the lilac
water laughing water squealing water pumping
the flowers turgid and full in bloom.

The Revolutionary

The dandies come at harvest
seize the swine, the grain,
the chickens with the grain
the fruit of the vine,
the vine itself from the heart of the earth
and I am grateful it is not more.

My potatoes rot in the landlord's dungeon.
My oxen feed spaniels and jackals.
Only they can sell the oil to warm my hands.
Feathers and claws are memories of food.
The earth swallows my blood and spits
clay and clods and one rusted sword.
The church says God hears
prayers of the righteous.
It is sin that keeps me poor.

What seems enough is never enough.
My sons, my sons
Where are my sons?
Tax for ambitions of flame and metal.

I will come through your jasmine window
with a rusted kiss
sharper than any patriotic lie
and in that harsh instant forge a thorn.

What the Cat Knows

When Sonny was dying,
the cat knew all about it,
Even though the haggling had not begun
And every notion fancied otherwise.
Cats know the knead of flesh, heat ebbing and rising
the furnace of cells that growls and grumbles.
The cat knows how tissues fragment,
how bones go astray,
how blood disguises clay in motion.

The cat knows distillations from the lungs,
scrys the trembling earth or a fribbling heart,
reads the colors of organs through a padded paw.
The cat knows solace is a simple lie too,
stretched and purring as if the heave and fro
of emancipation and extinction extinguished all bargains.

The Pearl

The seed of the gall grows
the mother of wounds, seasons
of tissue's rebellion sustained
by the sap of grinding
teeth and tumors of unsettled scores.

The psychic says it is flint at the tip
of the wedge, rinds of evidence
on the weighted beam, the compressed strata
that speak into dead center

and tilt equilibrium like a homeless coat of many layers and
layers of unwashed sweat, layers of patterns upon the face
that bear witness to the mirrors of dread:
scabbed intrusions into the asylums of everyday sanity.

This bitter onion of scars,
thirsting for vengeance.
Any target will do: family, friends, hapless
passerby. God help him
if she's in the mood to strike.

Former friends witnessed the quick step
from bitch to berserk and hide
behind evasions. Even children know
but can't make themselves say it:
The shame of sunny rooms, calm colors
and wired windows.

The oyster alone knows fermentations
hidden from scrutiny by the laminations of darkness
nourished by venom, building micron by micron
an irridescence of suppressed screams.

LaVergne, TN USA
22 October 2009
161666LV00003B/207/P